Stage Your Home For Profit

Book and DVD

Created by

Peggy Selinger-Eaton

Written by

Gayla Moghannam

Published by Eaton-Moghannam Publishing, Danville, California

www.peggyscorner.com

Cover design and graphic art by Susan Prang of Creative Eye

DVD music by Nicole Dionne of Primal Scream

ISBN: 978-0-9761660-09

Peggy's Corner, Inc
696 San Ramon Valley Blvd, #214
Danville, CA 94526
935.743.1083

A Note of Thanks from Peggy

I am so grateful to be surrounded by loving family and friends.
Thank you to all of the Brokers and Agents
who have supported my work and the clients who
have asked to learn my Art.

Rick D'alessandro and Tom O'Stasik, you have been a great
source of continued support and I thank you both.
Sue Kuehn, thank you for inspiring me to develop my talents
in home staging. Jeannine Fadem, you helped
get this project started and I appreciate all of your
assistance. And, to Gayla, thank you for bringing my dream
full circle. You are all my angels and I am
blessed to have you in my life.

A Note of Thanks from Gayla

To Kevin, Alyssa and Carli, for letting me redecorate our lives.
To Dee Simonelli for being a creative inspiration.
To Dan Vanatter, for bringing color and life to our book. And,
lastly, to Peggy for letting me be a part of this dream.

Stage Your Home For Profit

PART I

From the Outside, In

PART II
Staging the Rooms of Your Home

Chapter

PART III
Professional Touches

PART IV
Brokers Tour and Open House
125

PART V
Your Home Might Look Too Good To Sell
126

What is Home Staging?

Would you like to increase the value of your home by thousands, probably tens of thousands of dollars? Do you want multiple offers the day your home goes on the market? If your answer is yes, read on.

I'd like to share with you my secret techniques to easily and profitably prepare and merchandise your home for sale. In the Real Estate business, they call it home staging. I want to share it with you in a fun, easy to learn format. Along with this easy to read book, I have also included an instructional DVD.

Home staging is the process of preparing a home for sale. Through merchandising your goods, staging shows potential home buyers that your home is the best product available. Real estate experts know that a staged home sells faster and for considerably more money than one that is not staged.

The housing market is competitive. Home buyers demand solid products and home sellers demand top dollar. What a great way to satisfy both demands. By staging your home, you will be able to achieve a balance between a happy seller and happy buyer.

I've been staging and decorating homes for over eighteen years, with great success. My clients range from professional athletes, actors, and executives to every day people. The goals are always the same - to sell the home as quickly as possible at the highest price the market will bear.

I am excited to teach my signature techniques for using existing home furnishings to turn homes into warm and inviting places. These techniques make a small room feel large, an outdated bathroom look upgraded, and a boring family room look spectacular…all using your existing furniture and accessories. These techniques work and I've used them to stage over a thousand homes.

Take some of these ideas, or take them all— it's up to you. Since I can't see your individual properties, I'm giving you ideas from the thousands of homes I've staged. Some will apply to your situation and some may not. That's where you get to be the creative director. You create your own "wish list" or "profit list".

A "profit list" is an actual list of the changes that need to be made before selling your home. I used to call it a "wish list" until clients termed it the "Peggy Profit List". Small changes can make huge financial returns. Big changes can make gigantic returns. Your list might take a few days or a few weeks to complete. You are in control of the list and its outcome. Please copy my ideas; no need to re-invent the wheel.

In 2003, my daughter was in the market for her first home. Not having a great understanding of the housing market, she was shocked to see the difference between homes that I had staged versus other homes un-staged. I'll never forget her comment, "Mom, we walked into one of 'your homes' and could immediately feel ourselves as part of the home. We felt like we could drop our bags and belong." This feeling is why preparing and merchandising homes is so important. Good home stagers will offer potential buyers the experience of seeing themselves in your home.

Home Staging Basics

Through years of experience helping people buy and sell their homes, I developed seven major staging principles. These principles make one house sell immediately while the same home down the road stays on the market for months. Following these principles means your home is professionally packaged and presented, while creating maximum appeal and interest:

1. *Make a great first impression.*
2. *Maximize space and eliminate clutter.*
3. *Use light for an open, spacious feeling.*
4. *De-emphasize flaws.*
5. *Make your home appealing to buyers with varied tastes.*
6. *Create warmth.*
7. *Modernize.*

Most sellers straighten up their home, clean the carpets, turn all the lights on and hope for the best. Wait until you see how much more you can do to excite and charm prospective buyers!

Many times a Realtor will give the address of a new listing to a client so they can drive by and see if they might be interested in the house. A "drive by" should entice the buyer to venture inside. If they don't like what they see, they're on to the next house. This is why your home must have what Realtors call "curb appeal".

Home staging is more about what you should remove than what you might want to add. Is home staging expensive? Not at all. Will I have to buy new furniture or become an interior decorator to do it? Absolutely not. Everybody has things in their house that can create a clean and welcoming feeling.

Maximizing space is one of the most important principles of home staging. By removing all unnecessary or bulky items your home appears more spacious. Leaving just enough furniture and decorations creates a comfortable and inviting ambiance.

What if you decide, "My house is fine the way it is and I'd rather watch T.V. than read this silly book. Lots of people who've never even heard about home staging manage to sell their houses just fine."

That's like looking for a job without dressing for success or updating your resume. You'll probably get a job sooner or later. You might even be offered a decent salary. Contrast this to a well-prepared and polished applicant. You've tailored your resume to mirror just what the employer is looking for. Rather than pounding the pavement for a job that pays enough, you have the happy task of choosing among job offers and negotiating a healthy salary. A little effort ahead of time can sure make things easier in the long run.

Home staging will dress your house for success and emphasize the attributes that appeal to buyers. Like the job applicant who has done his homework, your house will stand head and shoulders above the competition. Highlight the positives of your home the same way you'd promote yourself to an interviewer.

In the same manner, de-emphasize the negatives of your home and accentuate the positives. No one needs to be hit over the head with freeway noise when the trickling sounds of a beautiful fountain can take its place.

Open House is like opening night. When the curtain goes up and that first buyer comes in the door, we want to knock his socks off with a house that far outshines its competition. Bright and cheery are words that describe everyone's dream home. So, turn on every light and lamp in your home to set the stage. Let them have amateur night down the street.

What do I mean by amateur night? Some amateur sellers would be the family who wants to display all of Jimmy and Jenny's soccer trophies, the lady who proudly shows off her 200 piece Smurf collection, or the fellow with the 30 foot prize ivy plant swallowing up the living room.

What's wrong with proudly displaying our hobbies or achievements? Nothing at all. I have two surfboards in my living room that I love. (Not really.) The point is how we live in a home and how we sell our house are two different things.

When you decorate your home, you want it to express your unique tastes and interests. Similarly, a prospective buyer is looking for a home that fits their lifestyle and personality. Since you can't possibly predict or reflect what each and every buyer would like, doesn't it make sense to broaden the appeal of your home so that almost anyone can picture living there happily?

Don't take it personally. Remember, selling your home is a business transaction. Even though you may be emotionally attached to the items in your home, now is the time to remove many of them in order to set the stage for the next proud owner.

Family pictures, religious items, trophies, and diplomas must go. Anything that hints of personal characteristics such as gender, race, nationality, sexual orientation, occupation, hobbies or interests should be removed. We want to help the buyer envision his or her individuality reflected by this house.

Home buyers know you have the right number of bedrooms and bathrooms long before they see the house. Your job is to make it easy for them to imagine their own taste and furnishings where yours are now. That's why another important principle of home staging is to make your house generic.

Generic is not the same thing as neutral. Your house doesn't need to be all white or all beige. We just don't want to overpower the would-be buyer with a color they dislike. By moving things around and removing all but the most necessary pieces, we can minimize the impression of a potentially offensive color.

Eliminating the colors you've worked so hard to repeat throughout the room when you were decorating may seem an odd thing to do, but I'm sure you can see the sense in it. Color is a personal thing, and we don't want to turn off a potential buyer.

Someone who hates red may just feel uncomfortable by your family room with the cute red couch and chairs. They probably wouldn't even be conscious of why they just don't "click" with your house.

Does this mean that you have to run out and buy a new sofa? Not at all. Keeping things generic in a home is as easy as splitting up the ensemble by putting the red chairs in another room. This is one way to minimize the "all red" impression. A well-placed throw blanket can also help to tone down distinct colors.

Creating warmth within your home is just as easy. Using your existing accessories, set the dining room table to resemble an elegant dinner, place a tea service on the coffee table, and put a bed tray on the master bed. These special touches will make your home feel warm and inviting to home buyers.

Maybe you're getting the sinking feeling that it might be too costly and difficult to stage your home. Who has the time or energy? Maybe you'd settle for a couple thousand dollars less just to avoid the hassle. Remember that your home is probably the best investment you'll ever make, especially when you factor in the tax benefits. A penny saved may be a penny earned, but a capital gain that could be tax exempt may also be worth double the money.

Before you turn your back on home staging, be sure you understand just how much easy money you may be walking away from. Not only is your house an investment that grows with time, the first $250,000 dollars of profit you make may be tax free. If you're married, the first $500,000 of capital gain may be tax-free.

Every thousand dollars of profit you can squeeze out of your house could be worth much more if you had to earn it and pay taxes on it. Factor in the money you save on your taxable income by taking a mortgage deduction and it becomes clear what a precious investment your home is. It just makes sense to showcase your house in a way that maximizes this tax-free profit.

By using the tested home staging principles described in this book to simply remove certain possessions in your home and rearrange the others, you can drastically increase your tax-free profit.

Even if you're in no hurry to sell your home, surely you wish to avoid the stress and hassle of straightening up and vacating the house every time a Realtor wants to bring by yet another look-ee-loo. The last thing you want is for your house to stay listed for awhile so people begin to wonder what's wrong with it or if you're desperate enough to accept a low-ball offer. Imagine the relief of having several fat full-price or better offers as soon as your house is shown!

A house that's been properly prepared is irresistible to buyers. Picture this:

John and Joanne Pre-qualified pull up to your house that has just gone on the market. A freshly painted mailbox in the front and some blooming annuals make a warm and welcoming entrance. The entry light is shiny and without cobwebs. Windows sparkle. The front door has a fresh coat of stain, paint or lemon oil on it.

The hopeful couple walks inside. Something smells delicious, maybe homemade cookies or freshly made cinnamon rolls. The table in the dining room shines with crystal and china set for an intimate and elegant dinner party. The kitchen table is brightly set for a picture perfect meal. The living room ottoman is ready for tea for two with an interesting book and a basket of fresh fruit. The beds are stacked with pillows, comforters fluffed and sheets folded back like the beds in Macy's linen department. Fresh cut flowers in vases are placed throughout the house and only a few large well-placed pieces are left to the rooms. The hallways are cleared of family pictures and the walls are uncluttered. Everywhere they look says bright, comfy and spacious.

Chapter 1
Make a Great First Impression

A prospective buyer's first impression is all-important.
It sets the tone for their expectations of the house. If the outside is a turn-off, they have already almost made up their mind about the house. There is much you can do to insure that their first look is pleasing and positive.

Approach the house with the eyes of a stranger.
Be honest. Stand in front of your home and take a seriously objective look. Pretend you've never seen this house before. Compare it to houses in architectural magazines and other neighborhoods. Look at your home from all angles. What is your first impression of the house? Don't take it personally. This is business. The better you are able to detach yourself from the experience, the more profit you'll make from the sale.

The front door and thresh should be in pristine condition.
Potential buyers will be waiting at your front door for several seconds while their Agent unlocks the door. This is where home buyer's first impressions begin. Make it a good one by dusting, painting, or power washing the door.

Power-wash where possible.

Inexpensive power-washers are readily available for purchase or you may use a professional power-washing service. You may want to have your driveway power-washed, depending on the surface. Difficult stains may be removed using dish washing liquid and, if all else fails, try coca-cola. Power-washing the sidewalk, driveway, front entry, and walkways make them look like new which makes your house look new. If your home's paint is cracked, and you are not going to repaint, then do not power-wash the exterior. This will only cause further damage to the home.

Eaves should be free of mildew and cobwebs, birds and bees.

Before

All windows must be sparkling clean.

The garage door should look clean and well painted.
Many of my clients have greatly improved the look and value of their homes by painting the garage doors and trim only. Sometimes this is all it takes to freshening up a home's exterior.

The mailbox must be properly maintained.
Mailboxes are inexpensive so consider replacing if necessary. Freshen paint, polish metal, and remove any vegetation as needed. Surround with flowers and bark if appropriate.

After

Painting is a good investment.

Sometimes painting the trim and gutters is all you need to give that fresh new paint look. If more than the trim needs painting, it will be worth your while to take care of it. Bargain Hunters are the only buyers who plan on moving into a house and repainting it. They hope to fix up the house with the atrocious paint in exchange for a generous savings on the purchase price. They know that the effort and money of painting will be well worth the investment. Let's beat them to it, shall we? You want and deserve top dollar for your tax savvy investment. A relatively small investment in paint can really boost your asking price.

Even if the paint is in good condition, you need to be objective about the color.

The color of the house can keep you from getting your best purchase price. Obviously purple or some other eccentric color must go, but did you know that brown can be almost as bad? Conservative home colors broaden appeal. So, stick to beige, taupe, camel, gray, or white. Update to a neutral color with trim in white, green, black, or camel and watch your profits go up.

Make sure your house number is clearly visible.
Can you read it at night?

A new doormat is crucial.
Buy one that is oversized and natural bristled. Mats should be larger than the actual size of the door. This gives the doorway a larger feel and look.

All light fixtures should be cleaned and shined.
Brass is outdated and should be replaced with iron, black, rust, brown, or white. A new fixture costs about nineteen dollars and is definitely worth the investment to update your home. Light fixtures may be painted if new fixtures are unaffordable. Work with your paint experts to select the proper paint.

Flowerpots should be placed at entry ways.
Home improvement stores sell pots of assorted flowers that work well. Two or three 12' to 16' containers of instant color flowerpots by the front door will really turn on the charm. The flowers in these containers should be matched in appearance and placed so as not to crowd the doorway. We don't want to make the entryway appear cramped.

Talk to your neighbors.
Boats that aren't in the water and cars that aren't in working condition on the street must be moved. Don't be afraid to ask for your neighbor's cooperation as it will benefit them to have your home sell for more money.

Chapter 2
The Front Yard

All grass areas must be green and free of bare spots.
Well manicured is the look we're going for. Fertilize the grass with a good nitrogen based turf builder to make it look lush and green. Apply fertilizer properly, taking care not to burn the grass. Use sod or seed as needed. And, don't forget to water, water, water! Sometimes weeds can be watered and mowed to look like grass.

Pruned bushes should be rounded.
Many gardeners and homeowners like to prune bushes into square shapes but when it's time to stage, we want a rounded look. A round look is more modern and pleasing to most people and gives bushes and shrubs a softer look. Hedges should remain squared, however.

Vegetation should not be higher than the fence unless it is strategically placed to hide an unsightly view.

Redwood and pine trees should be trimmed so that the bottom five feet of the trunk is visible.
Tree trunks are attractive and make the yard appear more spacious when properly pruned.

Fresh bark chips should be used to cover bare areas to create a finished look.
Invest in some new tiny black bark or regular bark chips to cover dirt that is easily seen. New wood chips really spruce up the garden and make it look professionally landscaped. I only use the larger chips and gorilla bark on hills or as a last resort.

Makes sure that all windows are clear of vegetation to allow maximum light into the home's interior.
An exception to this could be made if pruning would result in little left of the plant but dead wood.

Plant, plant, plant! Study your front yard.
In areas where the eyes are likely to rest, plant flowers in well-placed clumps. If your budget allows, flowers are a good investment and more really is better. Pink, purple, blue and white flowers are preferable. Try to stay away from yellow and orange flowers except during the months of September through November, reds in December. Don't plant flowers with a vision toward the future but for instant color when your house goes on the market.

Overlarge trees make a house look smaller.
If the trees and plantings are overpowering the house, the whole effect is dark and forbidding. You may love the giant old woody willow but if it's covering your house no one but the birds will want to move in.

All dead wood and underbrush must be removed.
We don't want prospective home buyer to think your yard is "neglected". This is the last thing you want people to think when they are comparing your house to other houses on the market.

Just as with the interior of the house, to get top dollar for our property, we need to make it look as spacious and manicured as possible.
All trees, bushes and hedges must look tended to and yards should appear open and friendly, not dark and forbidding. If it looks as though a witch, or a short, green Jedi master might live there, get out the pruning shears immediately.

Death to all weeds!
Remove all dead plants and trees, even those that will grow back next season. Remember, any dead wood should be pruned. Get rid of the lone bush that has no relation to the rest of the garden. Plantings should seem as though they belong together. An out of place tree creates disharmony.

If you feel that you can't be objective, invest in a professional opinion from a landscape architect.
Be ruthless! Beat back those jungle plants.

Chapter 3
The Backyard and Deck

The backyard should have a small seating area.
A home I just finished staging had a beautiful, lush lawn in the large backyard but there was nowhere to sit and enjoy it. The owners went out and bought an outdoor table and chairs and set it with a tablecloth, dishes and napkins. It was the perfect finishing touch.

Face all patio furniture towards the house.
Set up conversation areas but make sure they all face towards the house.

If weather permits, set the patio table with cups, plates and cloth napkins.

Missing a patio set?
Grab a fold out table and chairs. Cover with tablecloth and set with plates, cups and cloth napkins. No one will know.

Pack away kids toys and trampolines.
Swings, tree houses, sports court and basketball hoops are fine.

Power-wash the patio and decks.
Hundreds of my clients have restored their decks by power washing alone. The transformations are incredible. If necessary, consider having the deck oiled or repainted. Red paint on decks is outdated. Try beige and gray, instead.

Plant, plant, plant.
All backyards benefit from the beauty of flowers.

Use hanging plants in specific places to de-emphasize unsightly views or flaws.

Cover the BBQ if it's in questionable shape.
I like BBQ's. Just make sure they are not directly outside of the kitchen window or obstructing any views.

Keep it green!
Keep your lawn as green as can be. Use the same techniques of fertilizing and watering as in the front yard.

Make sure all trees and bushes are trimmed.
Clear away all weeds and dead brush.

Clean the eves of spider webs and dust.

Put down those umbrellas.
Umbrellas block the views of the backyard. They can be used strategically to de-emphasize any flaws in the backyard. Otherwise, put them down.

Chapter 4
The Pool and Spa

Clean your pool.
Make your pool look so inviting that all visitors want to take a dip.

Power wash the perimeter of the pool.
Years of suntan oil and backyard parties may have stained your pools patio.
A power wash will easily erase the years of fun and sun.

If safe, take off the porta-fence.
Only do this if it is absolutely safe for your family.

Get pool equipment in working order.
If necessary, consider emptying and refilling the pool.

Position all lounge chairs toward the house.

Deflate and remove floating chairs and water toys.

A rented pool fountain looks fabulous.
These are available at most pool supply stores.

Leave spas uncovered or folded back.
Sometimes, spas are located in odd areas of the yard. Don't let home buyers miss it. Throw 3 bright large beach balls into water to draw the attention of home buyers.

Turn on the bubbles.
It makes the spa look more inviting and soothing.

Chapter 5
The Pool House and Cabana

Make sure the pool house and cabana are clean.

Use vanilla plug-ins to get rid of the wet towel odors and make the pool house smell fresh.

Set out fresh towels in bright colors.
Hang them from the door and fold them over racks.

Consider painting the walls and cleaning the carpets.

If the pool house is used as an extra storage space, move the excess stuff to the garage.
A pool house may add value to any home as long as it is used as a pool house and not as storage.

PART II
Staging the Rooms of Your Home.

It's time to stage the inside of your house. Many of the techniques that follow can be applied to other rooms in your home. I encourage you to examine each room carefully and create a staging "profit list" of what needs to be done. I must warn you, however. Your house is going to look so good when you finish that you may not want to move! Just remember, staging is different than decorating. When staging, we are taking out furniture and accessories, not adding them.

Chapter 1
The Entryway

The entryway's wall color should be pleasing and coordinate well with the rest of the house.
Wallpaper is out and should be replaced with a more updated painted look. Color is important. Keep it as neutral as possible. If the area is small, use light colored paint.

Update your entryway.
If tiles in the entryway are poorly shaped or outdated in style or color, use a rug to minimize the effect. Brown, gold, rust, green, orange, and red colored tiles are undesirable. If possible, replace the floor with updated tiles or hardwood.

Coat racks should be left empty.
The leaning tower of coats must go. You might even find a few dollars in the pockets while you pack them away for the new home!

No shoe racks at the front door.
If you want home buyers to remove their shoes, try this trick: leave a pair of shoes at the front door. In California, most home buyers will see the stray shoes and remove their own before entering the home. However, this isn't always true in other parts of the Country. Do not leave a "remove your shoes" sign unless the carpet or flooring is brand new. It can offend home buyers.

Hide key racks.
Don't forget to pack away extra copies of house and car keys.

Replace brass and glass chimncy typc light fixtures.
If this is not possible, affordable lamp shades can be used to minimize their appearance. Inexpensive lamp shades can be purchased at home improvement and decorating stores.

Remove excess wall clutter, especially dried flower wreaths and family photos.
As a rule, mirrors are better than pictures. If pictures are to remain, they should blend into the background. No bright colors, modern, ethnic, or religious art. Less is definitely more.

A hall table and mirror work well for the entryway.
Realtor's cards and flyers may be displayed there.

A small votive candle may safely be used to warm and scent the entry.

34

Chapter 2
The Living Room

The living room needs to be a living room not an exercise room, office or game room.
Home buyers need to see a living room.

Carpet cleaning is a must for all homes.
If you have pets, apply the appropriate products to neutralize odors. Place furniture prior to having the carpets cleaned. It's okay to clean around the furniture if it's too heavy to move. There are carpet specialists who will repair specific areas by cutting out the damaged spot and replacing it with carpet recycled from an unseen area or leftover piece.

Before

After

37

Open window coverings and make the room look larger.
Bare windows are preferable to outdated or shabby window dressing.
Wood blinds are attractive; silhouettes, those very sheer fabric-covered blinds,
are better; wood shutters are the best and not surprisingly, the most expensive.
Metal blinds should be left open. Vertical blinds are very unpopular and can make
a home look cheap and outdated. The exception would be vertical blinds that are
similar to the silhouettes in fabric. These are very modern and popular.

If drapes are old, remove them.
I'd rather see sparkling windows than old dated drapes.

Fireplaces must be clean with real logs resting on the grate.
Hide the instant logs and candles! When weather indicates, a fire burning in the
fireplace creates a welcoming atmosphere. A framed mirror is preferable above the
fireplace but if that's not available a generic picture may be used.

**Living room furniture should be arranged in conversation
friendly configuration.**
The sofa facing the fireplace with a chair on each side and coffee table in the
middle usually works well but there are exceptions. Use your best judgment,
but do remember to keep the furniture at right angles! Although angling furniture
may be attractive, it does tend to throw some people and so it's best to avoid this
when staging. This is not a party, so don't line the walls with furniture.

Any unnecessary pieces of furniture or clutter should be moved to the garage.
Try to store things in an organized manner. Use a drop cloth or a moving dolly to
more easily slide furniture into the garage.

**Throws may be used strategically to minimize strong colors
or hide imperfections.**
I would encourage you to purchase an updated throw and new pillows. This can change the color and mood of the entire room at little expense. Sofa covers should only be used as a last resort.

A coffee table is mandatory equipment.
You can use stacking tables, a trunk, or ottoman if necessary to create the same effect. Set with two wine or champagne glasses, a decanter, two cloth napkins, a vase of fresh flowers and a candle to set the mood.

Unless your floors are tile are hardwood, remove throw rugs in the living room.
People think you are trying to hide something.

The living room is central to the buyer's first impression.
Leather sofas are too casual for the living room so use them only as a last resort. I highly recommend renting or borrowing furniture when necessary.

Chapter 3
The Dining Room

A dining room must look like a dining room.
It cannot be a home office, exercise or music room. A table and chairs are
mandatory! Card or patio tables can be disguised with table linens and no one
need be the wiser. Borrow or rent if needed.

**If you have a brass chandelier or lighting fixture in the dining room, or indeed
anywhere in the house, it should be replaced.**
If there is no option, disguise them with inexpensive mini-lamp shades
(see DVD for lighting examples).

**If there is a china cabinet with glass, take a significant amount of
extra items out of the cabinet.**
Normally, I use these items as centerpieces and decorations around the home.
Attractive and organized should be the end result.

Mirrors over credenzas help dining rooms look larger.

Set your dining room table.
No, I haven't lost my marbles. See Chapter "Setting Tables" and the
DVD for more information.

Plastic is great for ketchup bottles, not for floral arrangements.
I love the look of fresh cut flowers. As a rule, only use silk arrangements
younger than 2 years old. All plastic arrangements and greenery should
be moved to the garage.

Before

After

43

I'd rather see vintage wood than a tablecloth.
Pack away those tablecloths and let the wood shine through.
Besides, by the time you finish setting the table, the wood on the table
will hardly show.

**Remember that nothing is more central to staging your home than
removing inessential pieces of furniture to help create the
impression of more square footage.**
This includes the dining room so put the tea cart and
extra chairs in the garage.

Before

After

45

Chapter 4
The Family Room

The family room needs to be a family room.
Potential home buyers need to see a family room when touring your home.
If you were using the room as the twin's play area, borrow or rent a
sofa and coffee table.

A piano looks wonderful in spacious family rooms.
Tuck away the sheet music, top off with a candelabra or scented candle and
add a vase of fresh cut flowers.

Use stacking tables, a trunk, or ottoman as a coffee table, if needed.
Set coffee table with a teapot, two tea cups and saucers, two napkins, a small bowl
of five or so lemons, a vase of fresh flowers, and a pedestal type cake or
cookie plate arranged with tea cookies or petit fours.

**If your family room has a fireplace, furniture should be arranged to enjoy the
fire, not the TV.**
Try to create a conversation area that focuses on anything but the television.
No fireplace? If you have a beautiful view, then situate the furniture
to focus on the view.

Entertainment equipment and speakers should be minimized.
Staging isn't always practical. But, it is profitable. Remember this while moving
your large black speakers to the garage and putting the remotes under the couch.

No books or magazines on or under the coffee table, please.
If a coffee table book can be added without crowding the space, one medium to large picture book can be used. Be sure to consider the book cover's coloring.

Lazy boy chairs and recliners must go.
Most women dread the sight of lazy boys. Make your home appeal to everyone by moving lazy boy chairs and recliners to the garage.

Take away the throw rug under the coffee table unless flooring is hardwood or tile.

**Create warmth with the use of pillows, candles, minimal furniture,
and fresh cut flowers-not angled furniture.**
Staging is not the same as decorating. Moving furniture out of
angles will make your family room look more spacious.

Clean off bookshelves, mantles, and coffee tables.
I like to organize bookshelf accessories in bundles of three based
on themes and colors.

Live plants should be removed unless they are well pruned and in perfect shape.

Remove family photos.
For security reasons, I'd rather no one know who lives in the house. Taking your
family photos out keeps home buyers looking at your home and not the cute
photos on the wall.

Chapter 5
The Kitchen

Bar stools and a counter do not replace the kitchen table.
You must have kitchen table and chairs. As in our dining room example, a covered card or patio table serves as an adequate substitute.

Be sure to view my ideas on setting the kitchen table given in the DVD.
Set the tables so it is attractive but realistic: one glass (no plastic) per place setting, cloth napkins, and a fresh flower centerpiece.

Did I mention, counter top surfaces should be <u>completely</u> clear?
No microwave, toaster, blender, coffee pot, napkin holder, salt/pepper, rice cooker, bread maker, or dish rack. This creates the impression of more counter space and a sparkling clean kitchen.

To increase the selling price of your home, updating the kitchen is your wisest investment.
Replace old electric burners with a gas or flat top range if possible.
Gas is the home buyer's top choice.

Have your kitchen counters been around longer than the cockroach?
No problem. Easily update counter tops by repainting the grout. Bring in a grout specialist or visit your nearby home improvement store. White tiles must have white grout and gray tiles should have gray grout. As a general rule, the color of your grout should match the color of the tile.

No plants or items of any kind should rest atop the cabinets. None.

Do your cabinet doors have more chips than a bag of Lays?
Try painting them. Modernize by replacing brass knobs with chrome,
brushed nickel and iron handles. Your kitchen will look brand new.
(Yes, I even paint oak doors.) If you have wood cabinets,
use Murphy's Oil Soap mixed with hot water to clean
and Howard's Wax to polish.

Move half of everything in your cupboards to the garage.
We want home buyers to think your kitchen has enough space
for all of their dishes.

Sorry, your refrigerator is no longer your bulletin board.
Its surface should be absolutely clear—no magnets, calendars,
or photos whatsoever.

Only one garbage can per kitchen and it must be kept under the sink.
Trash compactors must be emptied frequently. Sponges, soap dispensers,
and the like also need to be stowed under the sink.

Pet dishes must be removed.

Remove excess storage cabinets and bins.
This gives the illusion of having adequate space in the kitchen for
all necessary appliances and dish ware.

Going, going, gone…hanging pots need to go.
So do dish towels, paper towels and paper towel holders.

If your kitchen floors are outdated, unattractive, or damaged, place the largest possible (within reason) area rug under the table and/or in front of the sink.
Replacing your kitchen floors? Pergo is my favorite choice for kitchen flooring. Simple patterned and neutral toned linoleum is my second favorite.

Move water dispensers to the garage.
They use up precious space within your kitchen.

Fresh fruit or vegetables make wonderful kitchen decorations.
Use one type of fruit or vegetable, depending on the season, and buy a lot of them. Place them in a large decorative bowl or vase. I love to use lemons, limes, artichokes or bell peppers.

Create a model home look by setting the table.
See Setting Tables Chapter and DVD for specifics.

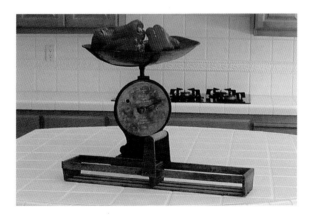

Chapter 6
The Bathroom

**If bathroom light fixtures are dated
(brass with celebrity bulbs), and they probably are, replace them.**
It is very inexpensive and can change the look of the entire bathroom.
This is most important for the master bathroom. If the fixture cannot
be removed, consider painting it. Work with your paint experts to
choose the best paint for the job.

Towels must be fresh and new.
New bath and hand towels should be displayed on the towel rack.
If space allows, roll three hand towels and place in a basket next to the sink.

**Be sure and remove <u>all</u> toilet items from the bathroom and
place in a basket or zip bag under the sink.**
This includes toothbrush holders, lotions, soap dishes and Kleenex boxes.
If in doubt, move it out.

A vase of fresh flowers on the counter top looks beautiful.
Set out a large fragrant candle on a candle dish. Make sure the candles
fragrance doesn't conflict with any other fragrances used in the house.

Bathroom grout must be pristine or refurbished.
Home improvement centers offer how-to kits, or professional grout experts
may be used. Definitely consider re-caulking the tub and sink area.

Old counter tops can be easily updated by painting out the grout.
Similar to the kitchen, the grout should match the color of the tile. Brown grout
with white tile is outdated. White tile must have white grout.

Chipped vanities can be updated with a fresh coat of paint.
Consider replacing vanity knobs to help
modernize the bathroom without remodeling.

I'm a firm believer in new shower curtains.

Replace decorative toilet seat covers and remove contoured toilet rugs.
New rugs should be placed in front of the sinks in all of the bathrooms unless they are carpeted. Rugs help de-emphasize outdated floors.

**Donate all bathroom reading material to the local library
(or move it to the garage).**

Remove or hide toilet bowl cleaners, plungers and wastebaskets.
Consider using plastic or paper trash bags instead of wastebaskets.
This makes it easier to remove the trash when potential clients
come to view your home.

Chapter 7
The Bedroom

Remove all posters, toys, pictures, trophies, and crafts.
One or two attractive stuffed animals may be used to decorate,
but they should be large in size.

Diaper pails should be undetectable by sight or smell.
Changing tables should be completely emptied of supplies, clothes, toys,
decorations, etc. It might be nice to have a small table and
chair or doll house in the room.

Teenage kids taught me to hide items under the bed.
This is a great place to hide alarm clocks and phones. Take all items off night
stands except lamps. This includes Kleenex boxes and glasses.

Store all personal photos.
Again, for security reasons, we don't want anyone to know who lives in the house.

Need a bed for the bedroom?
Blow up an air mattress, place it on top of 2 boxes and cover
with an attractive bedding set. No one needs to know it's not a "real" bed.

Keep bedrooms simple.
Bedrooms should have a bed, nightstand, dresser and lamp. Tidy bedding
and a vase of fresh flowers completes the look.

Wallpaper, drapes and comforters must coordinate.

Put closet doors back on the hinges.
If lost, order new ones. As a last resort, put up a cute curtain.

Carpeted rooms don't need rugs.

Mirrored closet doors modernize a room.
It also gives the room a more spacious feeling.

A stored crib will turn an empty room into a child's bedroom.
A retired client of mine brought in a 20 year old crib to turn a
spare room back into a bedroom. The room looked adorable with
the neighbors borrowed bedding. She thought I was crazy until the home
went on the market and sold in 3 days for thousands over the asking price!
Home buyers want to see bedrooms.

**Robes, ribbon holders, and hampers hanging from the back of
door need to be packed away.**

Chapter 8
The Master Bedroom

Coordinate master bathroom towels with your bedding.
Make sure the color scheme flows between the master bedroom
and master bath.

Clean out the closets.
9 out of 10 times potential home buyers will open the closets in the master bedroom. Therefore, the closets need to be immaculate. Take out all unnecessary clothes and shoes. Organize the closet by pants, shirts, skirts, and dresses. Go back and color coordinate. Your closet should look like a rack at Nordstroms. Clean off the top shelf of the closet. This area is reserved for baseball caps or hat boxes. Nothing else. Your closet needs to appear spacious.

Single women should put men's clothing in the master bedroom closet.
Clients will borrow men's clothing and shoes to place in their closets. You never know who is touring your home. Better safe than sorry.
A few items will do the trick!

Remove all items except lamps off of the night stands.
Alarm clocks, tissue boxes, telephones, books, glasses, etc. may be stored under the bed for easy access until the house is sold. This includes Kleenex boxes.

**An up-to-date and inviting comforter creates the atmosphere
we need in the master bedroom.**
Comforters should be turned back about twenty inches or so.
A bed-skirt and three layers of pillows complete the look. Bedding is
especially important in the master bedroom.

The bed can be the central point of vision for your master bedroom.
See "How to Make a Bed" for specific details.
I like to decorate the bed with a breakfast tray, tea set or champagne flutes,
napkins and a bud vase. Place a vase of fresh flowers and a scented candle
on the dresser.

Stuff it…under the bed that is.
Hide extra clothes, personal photographs, accessories, books, clocks, and the phone
under the bed. Who says hiding clothes under a bed is only for kids!

Mirrored closets look fabulous in master bedrooms.
Make the master bedroom look larger and more spacious by adding the gorgeous
reflections of a mirrored closet.

Chapter 9
The Office

The desk should be cleared off.
Take everything off except the computer and lamp.
Put away the stapler and desk set.

Have you been collecting mismatched office furniture from the .COM bust?
Keep the desk and move everything else to the garage. Remember, staging is different from decorating. If in doubt, take it out.

Computers, printers and fax machines are okay.
If possible, move metal filing cabinets to the garage.

If bookshelves are present, keep them half empty.
Remove all paperbacks leaving only the hardbound books. Organize shelving accessories in bundles of three and separate by theme and color.

Push books to the back of the bookshelf to give the room a larger feel.
When decorating, the books come forward in the bookshelf. But, when staging, push them to the back of the shelf. Arrange books from tall to small. This helps the bookshelf appear more organized.

Remove any plastic runners from under the desk chair.
Create warmth by exchanging the ergonomic chair with a covered chair from Pier One or Target.

Sometimes, I will leave a large book open on the desk.
Coffee cups and napkins with stylish eyeglasses complete the look.

It's okay to use hunting, fishing, and golf pictures in the office.
Remove all diplomas, schooling certificates, awards from the walls. Remove all personal photographs.

Your real estate agent will advise you of the items that should be moved to a secure location during the sale of your home.
Old watches, signed baseballs or sports memorabilia should be hidden if small enough to be stolen from the house.

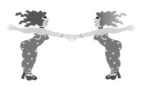

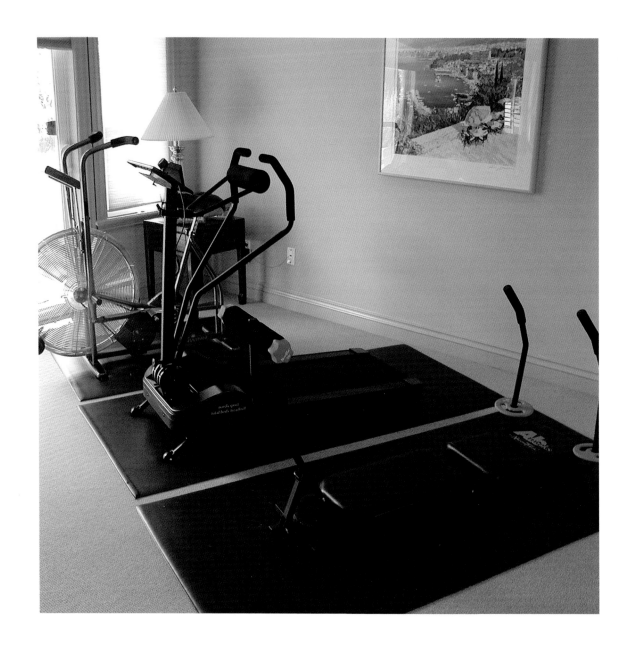

Chapter 10
The Exercise Room

Consider turning the exercise room back into a bedroom.
Many homes would benefit from an extra bedroom. Make sure
the exercise room is not in the middle of the living room,
family room or bedroom.

Remove all clothing, shoes, and old sports bottles from the exercise room.
Store these items in the garage to prevent odors from accumulating.

Plastic mats under exercise equipment should be removed if cracked or torn.

**Store signed baseballs, jerseys and other sports memorabilia in the garage
if small enough to be stolen.**
Your Agent will advise you further on this topic.

I like to put a towel over the handrails of the exercise equipment.
Sometimes, I'll move a TV from the children's room to the exercise room.
It gives the area a luxurious feeling.

**Put vanilla plug-in or deodorizer in the room
to make it smell pleasant.**

Chapter 11
The Laundry Room

Leave the washer and dryer.
Everything else goes. Keep the laundry room completely plain.
No detergent, no clothes, and no clotheslines. Now and then a cute
picture might be present.

Turn on the lights in the laundry room when showing.
A pretty rug will downplay outdated and old tile flooring.

**If your laundry facility is in the garage, put a rug in front of the
washer and dryer.**
No one likes to step on cold cement while doing laundry.

Try a screen.
I am staging a home that has a laundry facility in the garage. I put up a
screen to divide the garage and laundry machines. The screen encloses the
facility to make it look separate from the garage. It makes the area look
more friendly and welcoming. Sometimes, people feel uncomfortable doing
laundry in a garage, for fear of bugs and rodents. So, the investment of a rug
or screen turns fear into friendly.

Set out a beautiful laundry basket filled with rolled towels.

Chapter 12
The Bar

Pour yourself one last drink.
Then pack away the booze. Wine, spirits and beer all need to be packed out of sight. Leave decanters, ice bucket and crystal glassware.

Don't forget to remove the bowl of matches, stack of coasters and jar of swizzle sticks.
Martini shakers and bar gear should also be cleared off the counter top.

I've seen fun cork collections on many bars.
If your collection is just as great, keep it out. Just promise you'll hide all paper napkins and airline freebies.

I enjoy staging a bar counter with beer steins and cloth napkins.
I've also left a nice bottle of wine in an ice bucket with candle and cloth napkin. It's a great finishing touch.

Decanters look fabulous on any bar.
So do crystal glassware. Wash them to a sparkle and enjoy the brilliance.

Chapter 13
The Game Room

Game rooms are very popular.
More and more homes have game rooms. Show them off by
uncovering the equipment.

**If you have a pool table, uncover it and set with
2 cue sticks and racked balls.**
Place a tray set with 2 beer mugs and 2 cloth napkins next to the balls.

A ping pong table works fine in a game room.
If you don't want to purchase a pool table, use what you've got.
A bridge table can also be set up with cards.

Keep wall hangings simple and minimize any clutter in the room.

Bistro tables with coordinating stools look adorable in game rooms.

Turn on all of the lights in the game room.
This includes all game table lighting. Forget setting the mood of a
speak-easy. Go for bright and cheery.

**Eliminate smoke and cigar odors by cleaning carpets
and using vanilla plug-ins.**
See Odors chapter for more information.

Chapter 14
Theater and Entertainment Rooms

Leather sofa chairs with independent controls work well in theater and entertainment rooms.

The walls in the theater room should be freshly painted in a dark color.

Keep the room well lit while selling.

Leave the TV on with the sound off to highlight the features of the room.

Popcorn machines and soda machines can stay.
I like to set out a tray with soda bottles, cloth napkins, and a big bowl of popcorn.

Chapter 15
The Basement

If decorated properly, the basement can look like another room of the house.
If the floor is cement, think about purchasing an inexpensive carpet. Stenciling and outdoor murals can be used to brighten up basement walls. Consider turning your basement into an extra living space like a family room, game room, exercise room, or extra bedroom. Rent or borrow enough furniture to finish off the look. Home buyers love to see rooms, lots of rooms.

If the laundry facilities are in the basement, leave the washer and dryer.

Does your basement look like the local storage facility?
Consider moving boxes to the garage and turning the basement into an extra living space.

Pool tables and sports tables look terrific in the basement.

The basement stairway should be clean.
If necessary, paint and/or dust the stairwell.

Chapter 16
The Wine Cellar

Wine Cellars are very popular.
If there is any place in your home that could be altered to resemble a wine cellar (such as the basement) do it.

Larger wine cellars look spectacular with a bistro table and chairs set with bottle of wine, two glasses and two cloth napkins.
Sometimes, I will place a vineyard themed picture on the wall outside the door so people don't pass it by.

Stack boxes of wine as neatly as possible or out of sight.

Chapter 17
The Garage

Generally, people don't care too much about the garage.
They may peek in but that's about it. Sometimes a man will look to see if there's a workbench in his favorite hiding place. Feel free to use the garage to store all that great stuff you've pulled out of the house.

Avid car and motorcycle collectors typically keep garage areas tidy.
Straighten up tool table and equipment. Don't worry about the rest.

**Port-a-storage companies can help ease the pressure
of an over stuffed garage.**
They will drop off containers for you to fill. Then, they will transfer the items to a designated storage facility. See you local phone book for listings of companies in your area

Chapter 1
Odors

Beware of cat, dog, unusual cooking spices, and smoking odors.
It may take up to a month to eliminate these smells.

Time is your best weapon.
Smoke odors can be tough to erase. Give yourself the necessary time for the odors to dissipate. Clean your carpets, drapes, linens, air filters and clothing. Remove all ashtrays and clean up butts. Temporarily smoke outside or in the garage.

If you use pungent spices, store them in airtight containers or in the garage.
Clean the cabinets, floors, and stove top to remove spice residue. Sometimes drapes need to be cleaned or replaced.

Paint.
A fresh coat of paint is your best defense against unusual odors.

Febreze and other fabric sprays do wonders.
(Read the label for fabric limitations.)

Candle manufacturers make cookie and pie fragranced candles that smell like the real deal.
If you want the same affect, keep a bucket of frozen dough in the freezer and bake them when your house is open to buyers.

Tuck away pet dishes, beds, and blankets.
If possible, animal owners should consider sending pets to Grandma's house for a vacation. Dealing with a move can be an emotional time for both pet and owner.

If you have animals, make sure all pet stains are cleaned up.
This includes areas of the yard that the animal frequents.

Don't forget to clean and remove the diaper pails.

Clean walls around the toilet if excessive amounts of urine are present.
A solution of hot water and bleach (make sure this solution is safe for your walls) works well.

Don't forget to take out the trash daily when your home is on the market.

**Avoid the musty smell of a vacant home by strategically placing
a few plug-ins around the house.**

Antiques and older furniture can give off odors.
Try topping off the furniture with scented candles or moving the items
to your garage.

Get a little fresh air.
Open up your windows and enjoy the fresh air. It's free and effective.
Coordinate the fragrances of your plug-ins, candles and deodorizers.
Make sure the scent isn't too overpowering. (I only use vanilla.)

Chapter 2
Noise Control

Live near the freeway?
A fountain with a large drop can be used to distract from undesirable traffic or other outside noise. Fountains used for this purpose work well by the front door and in the back yard.

When you are showing the house, elevator or "easy listening" music should be played.

Noisy neighborhood?
Close the windows.

Chapter 3
Lighting

Light the place up.
Staging is the not same as entertaining. Turn on every single light, lamp, and chandelier in your home. Brighter is better.

Energy saving bulbs make your house appear dull and drab.
If you are using these, please change them. The traditional light bulb gives off a stronger and more attractive light.

Put the brightest light suggested in all of your fixtures.
Go through entire house and change all "mood" lighting to more sunshine light.

Make sure all rooms have enough lamps.
Borrow from neighbors or family, if necessary. All the lights should be turned on when people come to see the house, even in the daytime. The lighting will make your home appear cheerful and bright, especially in the evening or during the winter.

Old, yellowed, or dust ridden lamp shades should be replaced.
If you have lamps with dated shades (for example: accordion style shades), visit your local home store and swap them out. You can also transfer shades from other existing lamps. Kmart and Target are great lamp shade sources.

Remove the plastic protector shields from lamp shades.

Mother Earth gave us the best lighting of all.
Pull the blinds and open the shades. Let the good ole' sun shine in.

Clear away any plants or brush that block natural light from entering the home.

Remove window screens.
De-emphasize the flaws of older windows by removing the screens. Put them in the garage for the new owners and give the windows a good cleaning.

Chapter 4
Cleaning Your Home for Open House

Sometimes it's better to bring a cleaning service into your home.
It can be hard to be objective about dust and dirt. If you do bring in a cleaning service, bring them in before you stage your home. It can be frustrating to have your cleaning service move your furnishings after they have been carefully staged.

Clean all carpets.

Use Howard's Wax to give all woodwork that new shine look.
Put a quick coat of Murphy Oil Soap mixed with hot water on all woodwork such as, front doors, cabinets, tables, etc.

Don't forget to clean the following:

- Interior and Exterior Windows

- Furnace Returns

- Light Switches

- Baseboards

- Chandeliers

- Glass on Shower Doors

- Stairway

Before

After

Chapter 5
What To Do With a Vacant Home

**I believe it's very important to rent or borrow
furniture for all vacant homes.**
If no furniture is present, then potential home buyers will only have the
flaws in your home to look at. Furthermore, they may think you need to
sell your house in a hurry and offer you less money.

**At a minimum, rent or borrow living room, dining room and
breakfast nook furniture.**
If money allows, rent furniture for the family room and master bedroom, too.

A room that is particularly small or awkward cries out for furniture.
For example, one home I staged had a small master bedroom with a ghastly
view from an unusually small window. I rented a queen mattress, two night
stands, and two lamps. Make sure you top off the ensemble with
an appealing bedcover, dust ruffle, and pillows. Voila!

For beds, you can use air mattresses placed on boxes.
Again, make sure you top it off with attractive bed linens.

**If your house is vacant, it can be difficult for home buyers
to visualize where furniture should be placed.**
I just staged a 2200 square foot vacant home with rented furniture
for the living room, dining room, family room, and kitchen.
Family room furniture is especially important if it
is a very small room.

Put vases of fresh flowers and clean rolled towels in each of the bathrooms.
Use rugs as necessary.

You can negotiate one to three month contracts with furniture rental companies.
I've had great experiences with Brooks Furniture in California. I prefer to rent furniture for two months. One month is the most expensive. Three months is cheaper. Two months is a happy medium.

Use your plug-ins.
Vacant homes can smell dusty.

Chapter 6
Hobies and Collections

Keep all collections to a minimum.
Less looks better. Recently, I staged the home of an avid hunter.
We had to move Bambi, his stuffed friends, and the guns that killed
them out of the house. Of course, we made sure they were
safely packed away in the garage.

**Anything similar to a Beanie Baby or Precious Moment collection
should be packed up and stored for its new home.**
The same goes for GI Joe, Star Wars, and
stuffed animal collections.

**Quilt collections look especially beautiful when stacked on
a sewing machine, used as bedding, or as a tablecloth.**
I love to use quilts in a home. However,
I never use more than 3 in a home.

Are you an orchid lover?
Me too. You can keep your blooming orchids in the home.
Just remove the dormant plants.

**Sports collectables like signed balls, bats, and jerseys
should be removed if they can be easily stolen.**

CD's and videos should be stored out of sight.

Chapter 7
Animals

Remember to remove all pet dishes and bowls.
Move all animal beds, cat hotels, cat boxes, toys, and scratching posts out of sight. The garage is perfect for these types of items.

Kitty's litter box must go.
Make sure that all pets are put in the garage or moved to a friend's house during the showing of your home. This includes dogs, cats, exotic snakes, mice and hamsters.

Why is it that dogs have a heightened sense of smell and their owners the opposite?
If you have pets, use vanilla plug-ins to eliminate the smell.

Clean carpets.
If urine is present in the carpet, you should replace the padding and/or floorboards as well as carpet. This can cost as little as $75.00 a stain.

Reptiles can be scary to home shoppers.
Set up a new home for them in the garage. The same goes for rodents.

Having trouble putting "Rosco the Reptile" in the garage?
Tuck him behind the couch in a clean cage.

Fish tanks are okay in a sparkling clean bowl or aquarium.

Grab the shovel.
Clean up the area where your pet frequents.

The skittish cat that hides under the bed when anyone comes into the home is okay to keep indoors.
Just make sure it's safe for her to be around people and opening doors.
Don't forget to let your Agent know.

Pets like vacations too.
Consider giving a trip to Grandma's house, the neighbors or a pet hotel
until it is safe for them to be back. Pets can be emotional
about moving, too.

Chapter 8
Floral Arrangements

The dining, kitchen, living room, coffee table, kitchenette, and master bedroom should all be topped off with fresh floral arrangements.
Spring bouquets from your local grocery store will work.
In California, I love the arrangements found at Trader Joe's, Safeway, Costco, and Sam's.

Always use real flowers.
No dried or silk. Except for special arrangements that are in perfect condition and modern.

Change vase water frequently to prevent unnecessary odors.

Flowers can help de-emphasize flaws by drawing attention away from the problem areas.

Use fresh vegetables and fruit as centerpieces.

Silk floral arrangements are okay to use if you will be absent during the sale of your home.

Chapter 9
Setting Tables

In the dining room, I prefer to have six place settings with only four chairs.
This lends a less crowded yet elegant and festive look.

Crystal is wonderful.

A plate and bowl at each setting is ideal.
Complete the look with a combination of any fruit and vegetable. I like
to use pears, artichokes, lemons, Japanese eggplant, mangos, and any other
fruit that will last for a while. Place it on top of a handful of: rice, popcorn,
kidney beans, lentils, peas, dried cranberry, black beans, coffee, or navy beans.
Usually, I'll add a votive in the middle. See DVD for more
examples of table settings.

**Fresh flowers are a must for the dining
room centerpiece.**
I prefer not to use place mats or table linens. Chargers are a wonderful
addition to your best china. Silver, porcelain, iron or crystal candle
holders or candelabras are attractive as well.

Use safe candles.
For example, the small votive variety may be lit on the day of your
open house or brokers' tour. I like to set the tables so that the home
seller can move everything to the center of the table at mealtime
and then easily placed back again.

**Dining room place settings should include water,
wine and champagne glasses.**
Glasses don't have to be Waterford or even match, you want it to look like
a fun and festive dinner party is in progress.

Always use cloth napkins.
No paper or plastic on the table. Set the napkin inside of the wine glass or
water glass. See DVD for examples.

Matching plates, glasses and silverware aren't necessary.
Mix and match your existing sets. We're trying to create a feeling
of warmth, not impress the Queen of England.

If it is a nice day, set your patio tables.
Use a tablecloth, cloth napkins and non-disposable dishware.

Chapter 10
Making a Bed

**Three rows of pillows and an updated comforter will give any
bed the look of a showroom floor bed.**
Start at the headboard with the pillows you sleep on. Place Euro shams
next, followed by two king size shams. Finish with three small decorative
pillows. Use three Euro shams for a king size bed and two for a queen or
full. Pull back the flat sheet to meet the top of the comforter.

**Place a bed tray or flat tray on the bed with two champagne glasses,
two cloth napkins and a bud vase.**
You could also fill a basket with similar goodies.

You don't have to rob a bank to update your bedding.
Target, Kmart, Kohl's, and even the better department stores have great bed
sets for less. The Bed in A Bag variety is usually a good deal and stores like
Macy's routinely have comforter sales.

Before

After

Chapter 11
Window Coverings

I prefer the following window coverings in this order: shutters, silhouettes, wood blinds, and as a last resort aluminum.
All window coverings should be opened during home viewing regardless of the type. Vertical blinds are dated and should be removed, unless it is the silhouette type.

Window coverings don't need to be more elaborate than a rod and drape.
We are creating a sense of warmth. Don't spend a lot of money on your coverings. It isn't necessary.

If you have a view, don't worry about drapes.

Use blinds to minimize an unsightly view.
Close the blinds slightly so light may enter but the eyesore may not.
If you live on a golf course, all windows facing the course must have drapes.

Make sure all window coverings are dusted and cleaned.
Remove them if they are shabby, outdated, or overly colorful.

Pleated window shades in round windows are dated and should be removed.

Remove window screens on dated windows and store in the garage.

PART IV
Brokers Tour and Open House

Keep your home staged until it is appraised and all contingencies are removed.

Turn on every light in the house!
Don't forget your lamps!

Ceiling fans should be turned on low.

Elevator or "easy listening" music should be played.
Trust me, these people aren't ready for heavy
metal or gangsta rap.

Pull up blinds and open window coverings.

Light safe votive candles placed in strategic areas of the home.

Place fresh flowers in designated rooms.

It is always nice to have a dish of candy at the front door.

Take garbage, diapers, and cat litter boxes out of the home.

PART V
Your Home Looks Too Good to Sell!

Okay. You've made your wish list, followed through, and your home is staged and ready. If you are like most people, you're bound to look around and wonder why on earth you would ever want to sell this gorgeous house! This is definitely the downside to home staging but I'm afraid it can't be helped. All I can say is that the fat, juicy offers you're about to receive for your home will go a long way toward making you feel better!

Go ahead and put your feet up on the coffee table and take a moment to congratulate yourself for a job well done. Now you're ready for the doorbell to ring and the show to begin!